AT PORT ROYAL

T0151209

Publication of this book was supported by a grant from
The Greenwall Fund of The Academy of American Poets

AT PORT ROYAL

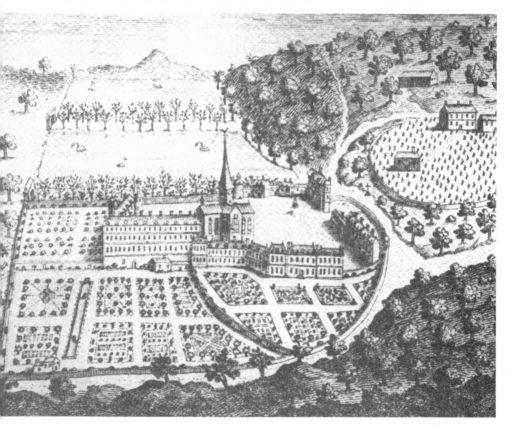

CHRISTOPHER EDGAR

ADVENTURES IN POETRY

Thanks to Amy Edgar, Trevor Winkfield, Olivier Brossard, Larry Fagin, Cris Mattison, Carol Conroy, Ezra Shales, Catherine Barnett, John Ashbery, Jordan Davis, Nancy Shapiro, Ron Padgett, Christina Davis, and the Fund for Poetry.

Some of the poems in this book appeared in the following publications: *Best American Poetry 2000, Best American Poetry 2001, Boston Review, Double Change, Explosive, Fence, Great American Prose Poems, Jahrbuch für Lyrik, Lincoln Center Theater Review, L'Oeil de Bœuf, Mississippi Review, Poésie, Poetry Daily, Sal Mimeo, Shiny, Skidrow Penthouse, The Germ,* and *Verse. Cheap Day Return* was published as a chapbook, with illustrations by Trevor Winkfield, by The Cube Press.

*

Adventures in Poetry titles are distributed through Zephyr Press by Consortium Book Sales and Distribution (www.cbsd.com) and by SPD: Small Press Distribution (www.sbdbooks.org).

*

Library of Congress Cataloging-in-Publication Data

Edgar, Christopher, 1961–
  At Port Royal / Chris Edgar.
      p. cm. -- (Adventures in poetry)
  ISBN 0-9706250-8-1 (alk. paper)
  I. Title. II. Adventures in poetry (Brookline, Mass.)
  PS3605.D455A93 2003
  811'.54--dc22

                                2003016726

07 06 05 04 03   9 8 7 6 5 4 3 2 FIRST EDITION
ADVENTURES IN POETRY
NEW YORK 🐞 BOSTON
WWW.ADVENTURESINPOETRY.COM

Front cover photograph: Ezra Shales
Design: Chris Edgar
Printed in Canada

CONTENTS

for A.E. *and* T.W.

Birthday

I have a confession to make:
When I was young
I was always losing shoes.
Of course, the climate was different then—
The trees both bigger and easier to climb,
The birds more virtuous,
More butterflies, fewer clouds,
And all around,
The smell of burning peat.
Blue men roamed the earth
Behind stone walls built by Romans
At the far end of our yard, where
The jungles of Southeast Asia began.
You see, I was a legionnaire sent to find the North Pole—
My brother was Horatio Hornblower . . .
No, we were all away when the zeppelin landed.
My father was magistrate in Khartoum,
Where my mother tended to the sick,
My brother had just befriended Niels Bohr
When I signed the petition to free Dreyfus.
Mata Hari lived next door—
It was her the zeppelin came for—
Like Baba Yaga she kept a shrunken head
On her front porch, with a lighted candle in it.
We all knew she worked for the other side
And ate Crusader flesh, she was a real pterodactyl.
That was the year the Nile overflowed its banks,
That Krakatoa, east of Java, sent the reek of
Burning cloves through the South Seas,

In Siberia a woolly mammoth skull was found
Under a mountain of ice on my tenth birthday
My brother was in bed with scurvy, and rickets,
And elephantiasis of the liver, and my mother gave him
Balms, and myrrh, and more balms and myrrh, and
mustard plasters, and I got a blunderbuss, a jaguar, and a
troglodyte, and we ate figs and eels and Baked Alaska and
drank grenadine straight from the bottle, we witnessed
the invention of gunpowder, saw gauchos lasso rheas
with bolas and drink maté, while natives buried fish in
the garden, with Marco Polo, and Good King Wenceslaus
pummelled Bad King John into submission until he saw
stars—Andromeda and Orion and Draco the dragon—
we made him ride over the Bridge of Assizes with the last
of the Hittites on a donkey, naked through the streets of
Coventry, Maximilian brought an aardvark to the dance,
and was summarily executed, by Savonarola, who stole
fire from the gods and tried to get away on the back of a
roc, and then on a juggernaut, only to cause Ragnarök,
the twilight of the gods; it was then, too, that Rasputin
danced with Mary Queen of Scots for the last time,
I can still see her sobbing into her mantilla....

Town and Country

Enormous shadow,
Release the sun.
Be gone and reappear
With the finesse of thirty years ago,
As Rita Hayworth,
The Flatiron Building,
Grand Army Plaza,
Crass waste places of Astoria,
On first sight a group of nature studies,
Shadows from commercial signs,
People on the street below
From the thirties and forties—
Pine needles, a moth on leaves,
A pine trunk, a birch tree—
Escapees from an Ansel Adams show—
Pictures of July afternoons
Outside the petting zoo,
An elderly woman eating ice cream
With the finesse of thirty years ago,
The Flatiron Building,
The Sheep Meadow,
Sailors in Times Square,
Signs in Times Square,
Sailors in Bethesda Fountain,
Figures in the piazza
All casting shadows

Through the long green
Tunnel of the Taconic—
Birches, pines,
Needles, moths, leaves—
Bull moose in a Maine lake,
Summer, 1971.

National Epik

Halfway to the nuthouse
The view to the southeast
Is all neat rowing boats
God bless them all
And also
The ruined pilgrim church

I.
In the midst of wild forest
The shade of birds follows
All changes of the panorama
The narrow straits change the open sea
A bathing resort becomes
The most southern terminus of the rail line
A university town home to hundreds of
Small taverns grinning wildly with silver
Winter sportsmen in fur caps at dawn
A modern park with wild ducks beside
A major river lined with parks and factories
A navigable boat-route   "the Poet's Way"
Situated on a neck of land between two lakes
A town the second largest sees evenings as
A mirror of sunlight   a pale blue lake
Surrounded by evergreen forests with mysterious caves

Here travelling judges held their courts
This prehistoric burial place was a fertile field
Gained by draining the tomb of a hero
The former lake bottom   a sandy shore

A traveller looks away from reindeer feels sadness
The old days trapped in a rival seafaring town
Helga's young daughters' corsets
Now frescos in a mausoleum
Early predecessors following the moving coastline
Continuously rising here now some seventy kilometers
From the old limestone quarry
They built and destroyed a bishop's castle
Many centuries ago a pleasant destination
All sunny cliffs hostels frequented by young people
The summer residence of the President famous for
Its monastery, now a popular bathing resort
Here a crane escaped an important fire
Arranged as a handicrafts museum
Oak forests and neo-classical buildings
Developed into a modern industrial center to protect
        the river-mouth
A main thoroughfare was buried in the apse of the cathedral

II.
Since medieval times our national epic was situated on
        a peninsula
A windy promontory
Stoically beginning the prosperity of nineteenth-century
        shipbuilding
Sticking out, all cliffs and sands
Over time this ugly duckling became
Fertile and rich, a popular bathing resort
Home to books and artists, salons
Idyllic hiatus of the national poet
Standing on rocky soil facing tempests a birch-path-

Embroidered monument to the National Theatre
A national dress of high standard even aesthetically
First impressions of the last decades in plain air
The Olympic Stadion   the central railway station
        majestic pine forests
Export the life of the people, the dominant force of livelihood
A new type of bath house
Steady and meditative even to the point of slowness
Spontaneous only in the midst of vast forest
The young prince, final heir to the royal blood
Eloped and lost
In the night, lone witness to
The fatal mistake of both
The last "Miss Europe" and "Miss Universe"

III.
In February the trees are shining
Like skiing terrains at their best
Old man and hammer celebrate winter
And the power of air is broken down
The horizon is illuminated
By the long night there are no clouds the sun is above
Fifty-one below, dangerous for the inexperienced traveller
Seems rather mild here, no polar bears walk the streets
All corresponding latitudes can be found only in
The zoological garden
A vivid landscape of purple, yellow, and red where
Dusk is not gray but tinged with shadowless lightness
Far off, one can see
Endless stretches of fir-forest and silver lakes that fail
To reach island-embroidered sky

Tops of mountains separated by winding channels
A blue-green carpet equally labyrinthine reawakening
  nature
In its chilling embrace the ancient rock night and morning
  lapse
Back and forth, a bridge crosses the confluence of two
  major rivers
Main streets are cut by cross-streets to form again
The octangle home of the military college
The famous waterfall   the hydro-electric station
Banks and locks, aspens and birches
All blown up by the Russians
The timber industry totally destroyed
The water tower one of the few landmarks
To have escaped destruction by fire
Narrow streets lined with houses
Now conform to a rectilinear plan
A stretch of sand, a trading place and fortification in the
  Middle Ages
Said, in time of war, to be beautiful and varied
Especially during the summer solstice, braised over an
  open fire
Two whole nights above sea level travellers gather
At the polar circle, a popular bathing resort
Excellent for walking tours good food for lodging
Chains of hills rich in white sand lakes and islands
Kilometers where only reindeer wander
Backwoods where the grunting bear lurks
Excited rambling for two days along paths mysterious
Melancholy highways and arable lands worth seeing

Near to railway connections reached only by air
Converted heathens are baptized at the north end of a lake
A cloth is spread out on the windward side of a log-fire
Reached only by the belt of a dwarf
Yielding to virgin pine forests on the lower slopes
Just once a year, at midsummer, the lake is
Eighty kilometers wide and forty kilometers long
To understand this junction of our most northern highways
This paradise of sports fishermen
A man must spend the night with a bear
An imposing experience, cold and windy
Wear plenty of clothing and a good waterproof
As in a dream, a small house between the river and
The falls, covered with felt and turf every now and then

IV.
O northernmost meteorological station
In the middle of the lower picture off to the right
Open to the eye of the traveller
"La route des quatre vents"
Can only be reckoned among the most magnificent
Characteristic and respectful of the rugged beauty
        of others
Half-wild, divided into herds, sometimes gathered into
        enclosures
A feast for people from the south and an interesting sight
Winter can be a rare and bizarre experience
The pleasure of skiing
Makes the journey longer   the cottage necessary

A constant dazzling play of light and shade
Soon to be replaced by cloud-shadow
Tinted pale rose   valleys lost by the last sun-rays
Fisherman and hunters
May be dark blue   shining   white   dark
Lost in twilight

Lost and Found

We looked all through
The Pripet Marshes
But couldn't find Jack
So skirting the plunging neckline
And buffeted by the warm south wind
We came to in the hanging gardens
Wherein the damp porch with
Its upas tree stood, and blossoming jacaranda

Life was good there in the highlands
On second thought second to none
Entirely silent, a silence of lank nothingness
Shot through by holes
All weight fell out through them
In unison, one could quietly exhale
Light a cigarette and watch it burn

We came to a parapet
Then came to lapse on a spur
Somewhere a paper door opened
Out flew a wild duck
An unseen illustration
Bisected by flares
Vertigo in symmetry
Artillery in the night sky
Martens in the soft forest
Orange boxcars in the surf

Darlings of the verdigris
Islands enmesh
The vertical plain
The hinterland's stilted burning bush

In C

Loosen focus, trees move. A weekend becomes a fortnight. Aspects of leaves float supine, assume the horizontal positions of pirogues and barques skirting air. Greasy plaits and tiny shoulders form the outline of a young girl. Reverse perspective and the basic facts become memoirs of an amnesiac lost among nuns. These exercises are clear from the verandahs of the modest bungalows dotting the peninsula. Natives dream in bergamot and bougainvillaea. And why not? Let it slide. The life of forms in art is short, pathological then normal, the distance between which the eye abolishes. An awareness of surface covers the dirty dog which is in fact curved, and we are all oriented toward a single point, skating harpy-like down a rivulet of pond scum to a spiral jetty in a giant ravine. Here the placid lake lay, until discovered upside-down in the 1840s by a group of brown studies. Some years later, Dirk "Poussin" Bouts halted discourse and the vanishing axis rode off into the sunset. Evidence of cause and effect was ample, a staircase the foreshortened River Jordan must climb. Painterly waves converged into a plastic and solid mountain of water that in fact framed him. Enraged, he created a doctrine reflecting optical unity. Man-mountains became mountain men, and "water mountains" became bodies in space, "space boxes" tied together for better or worse, richer or poorer, with scotch tape. The necessary verso of the entire plane became largesse, weather became more clement, a hollow body made of felt, mutatis mutandis, as with an uncertain decisiveness he shimmered forth toward the flat bank, behind which she disappeared on a funicular.

Pint-sized Lilliput

Standing on a bridge,
She guides shipping with her hand,
Without pictures or conversations,
A girl
Connecting two islands and the harbor
Teaches future skippers the way of ships.
Her movements are eddies in mindless flow,
Notoriously clean and selfless,
Her pause oppositional to
More ample evidence of the desire to keep up
With those Brobdingnagian boys
Smartly up-to-date in every detail,
Little movie fans buying bargain tickets.
Just a step away, she kisses the knee-high lighthouse,
Causing all age differences to disappear—
The more the railway follows the landscape,
The more the posed cattle promote the illusion of reality.
No one wants to hurry;
The rhythmic hee-haw of busy saws
Draws steady "oohs" and "ahs" and surges of electricity.
The citizenry can relax on tidy lawns,
Weary little urbanites who see through
The whole disguise,
The wrong end of the binoculars—
What is the use of a book?
The old waterwheel turns. Hikers and dogs pause
        to watch

The wheel go round and the miller
Carry in a bag of grain.
Scarcely a flea-jump from High Street
A commodious hotel with cocktail bar beckons comforts
To a tiny transient no larger than a cookie dish.

To the Antipodes

He had no truck with her,
Or so it seemed, at the scene
Of the accident, as we left its jurisdiction,
Mid-sentence, mid-cloverleaf,
Entering a demilitarized zone
Replete with palms,
Where, by a dry-dock in the rain,
There was once a shady glen.
There, one sphere of
Influence merged with another
To create something akin to
A spot on the sun.

It was a close shave
In the tin goose.
We might have bought it
Were we not invisible.

Instead we drew the blinds,
Thinking back on when
We last attempted to use the word
Yesteryear in everyday speech.
It must be time to go downtown.
Shall we take the parkway,
The expressway, or old U.S. 1?
But we are running late, and
A few too many things collide
In the free fall of the dumb waiter—
Coming of age riding the clutch,
Long weekends in small hotels,

Dog days of August, *The 49th Parallel,*
Trade winds, the Sargasso Sea,
Steamer to Montevideo, the odor of rain—
There is no telling my jetsam from yours,
As it were, in the gloaming.
The doctor gave me a tetanus shot
Because the dog really might have been rabid.
You see, the synapses still fire occasionally.
Like those tailors who rouse
Themselves from drunkenness
Just long enough
To take our money at cards,
We go west and south
To distinguish ourselves
At the same time to prove
Someone is home, a light is on.

The Reformation of Cities

Go blanket the greenbelt market garden
Search the forest for the ancient cummerbund
Kiss the coral sea goodbye
Shake hands with the new gardener
Use a long polecat in the wading pond
Flay a kite enamelled in a distant gaze
Get out from under this heavy template
Slightly giddy like a frontage road withstand
The brutal love of the plaintive estuary
Dispell, enfold the caution horses
Balance the safety matches
Leeward side of the severed cupola
Wage war with flecked ions
And extraordinary vapors
When night comes to cities of the plain
The land is dark and absent
A man climbing a mountain
Yodelling inside a silo
Artesian springs leak nebulae
All phantasmagoric, the humming circumflex
Laughs heartily along with
The structures of everyday life
Which build upon each other and rebuild
The construction of cities subsides
Hours turn on a gigantic plumb line
Dangling over an enchanting tarpaulin
Mesmer lost track of the beam here
Monument to lost dazzling religions

Fervor surged and bewildered
Airtight is the drum
Crows fly by at night

The Waning of the Play-Element

This tawny you is not you,
Living in the eiderdown
Hearing faraway motors sputter in the rain
While the woods
Amble along within
A notion of internal happiness.
Live in the desert long enough
And you develop strange beliefs:
That we are living inside a gigantic pun
That the universe is a constantly unravelling tutu
That limbs have minds of their own and will fly off
At the slightest provocation
That all is contained in the tension between
The magneto and the conundrum.
To set the watchspring in motion we must embrace
Not only you but everything we call
Play in the original dangerous passage.
We see the unsteady gaze of Mr. Chin,
Who decamps in peace. Shall we hem
Them in against the river?
Why not, since the victorious
Captain thrice surrendered there
To enemies of Spring? Without hesitation,
Max coldcocked the crow who sang
With all the pent-up silent fury of youth.
Punch-drunk, three resplendent kings
Reorient, and slowly find themselves
Deranged, taking flight
Inside the tawny you.

Petronius Arbiter

Small house and quiet tree
Grapes on the vine
Distaff elm and the little Dutchman
Pecking through the hard cherries
Ruining all the pears and apples
Shaking the olives out of Pallas's tree
And overwatering the soil
Those fields of kale
Those darned heavy creeping mallows
Weighing down my eyelids
Like so many smoking poppies
To go a-snaring for birds
Angling for the shy trout, timid deer
Go now, and ask the fields
To pay you back for all
You've done for them
Ingrate fields
I will go swimming

The Cloud of Unknowing

Is not a cloud at all
But a wall colored so efficiently
It seems to be an alley of trees
Some believe this cul de sac
Can be approached from every angle
While others consider it merely a frontage road
To the remnants of summer, the disused
Anchorage inside the spiral jetty
But we have seen this cloud, you and I have
Just before we set out to martinize the infidel
It was there, fifty miles south of Tripoli
Sometime in the late '50s, hovering above an Italian
    restaurant
Perched on the edge of a depression
White-tunicked waiters with jet-black hair served us
Canelloni and Chianti yet at the same time did not
Serve us canelloni and Chianti
We were at sea as we always were in those times
On a ferry yes the Dover ferry
Everyone was heaving
Patches of sawdust everywhere on deck
Always followed by the cloud
The sun came out but it was still raining
North of Leningrad the tramline ends
We trudge through acres of mud between
Grim apartment blocks in a colorless landscape
Day for night, whistling in the sleet
The mud becomes woods, beyond the woods

We finally reach the little wooden village on the far side
    of a hill
Bent-bark roofs as in the poem
With a little Orthodox church, a bit like St-Cloud
From a distance this is Old Russia I think
We meet the priest whom I like
Immediately we parted as old friends
Never saw him again
Funny, like the facial expressions of the father and son
Pickpocket team in the Mexico City subway
June rush hour you all of a sudden turn to
Shake their hands "¡Que pasa?!"
They looked as if they had seen a ghost
Probably like my own face when I lost my passport
In a dream. I was in Heathrow and hung my coat
On the convenient too convenient rack outside
    the duty-free shops
The Pakistani woman at the gate was very helpful
But could not help me
For some reason I was interested only
In which languages she spoke
The truth was all I wanted was for her
To say Urdu, which she did.

Norderney

after Shklovsky

Alya! You did a good job telling me about the ocean liner
If I bore you please inform me I will lay out my tiny heart
Like a man bent over a stone, sharpening a knife
Propulsion and anxiety, the interstices of
A conversation no one knows how to continue
Turns to a different brand of sorrow, one international
In scope, a book with no plot and few characters
Points in a landscape to hang one's hat on
Until a fried fish laughs in our literature for the first time
He who is strongest will have a good laugh
On a distant slope a flare or two an ambulance girl
A Saint Bernard with human graces an old brown felt hat
All worn out by the Spree a girl jumps rope
A Dixieland band plays trombone banjo ukelele
Because their tuxedos were old, they survived the
          revolution
Someone put windows in art, but others took them out
Alya, you're getting more pesky all the time
The water keeps rising
In Hamburg a beautiful automobile drives by
Are there such handsome cars in Moscow?
I doubt it

Possible Gothams

Though the building never ends
All we heard predicted has not occurred
Dreams of a Second Avenue subway linger on
As does the shadow of the Third Avenue el
Like a new Madison Square Garden each year
We recreate ourselves ten blocks further
Uptown, pausing only to see beautiful women
Walk pumas in the Ramble
Thinking of lunch, Luchow's or Lindy's, it all seems
Unfinished, as if there were no blueprint, and never was
More than one McKim, Mead, and White
There's a certain beauty to scaffolding and dust
And vertical games of musical chairs
Better to wake to the sound of a jackhammer
Than live in some toy town, some "Little Vienna"
And if someday it all becomes too much
We'll walk to New Jersey, over the landfills
Or hop an air taxi downtown

Gradual

This book of hours is piebald,
Each two alike only insofar as they are unalike.
Grass dies on the banks
As the waterways lie frozen. Piers
The Ploughman should be in the field
Sleeping with the other peasants,
But no, he is fickle and has gone to town.
The miller hoists another bag of grain
As his wife churns the butter.
Tiring, she opens a window and looks outside.
Trees sway gently in unison,
Stick-figures conferring on various topics of blue.
They are only doing what she asked them to,
Slowly, without prevarication, swaying gently in unison.
Centuries later, a woman
Turns her head and looks away.
A man, who loves her, becomes foreshortened:
Out of sorts, short of breath, and at a loss for words.
She thinks him too serious—
He must remember
That when the dog barks at midnight
It is only saying hello.
The woman is thinking of saints' feet in water.
The man is thinking of lives under glass,
Of how we are ourselves only when we are alone,
And of how we can sometimes be alone together.
The star above them looks down on them
And laughs, cruelly.
(Legend has it that there were two stars,

So the star, too, is not alone.)
The woman dreams of multicolored pylons,
Of woolen buildings, and people who are like
Woolen buildings, a raft of woolen buildings
Cast adrift on an empty sea.
In a dream the man attends a concert
Given by a Peruvian dwarf, who sings
Of vast Peruvian deserts by the sea.
Between the two lies a kaleidoscope,
A list pages long
Of things that could lie between them,
Patchworks of angry basilisks
In an empty landscape,
Endless tundra, a large country
Where there are Mounties
Because there are Nazis in the Rockies.
This nightmare of his is a film
From which he must now awake.
It is stiflingly hot. He opens a window
And breathes the cool night air flooding in
From the zoological garden. He decides to write
An opus, a treatise on how we are all trapped,
Animals in a zoo without love, from
Which we will escape, sometime in a later chapter.
The next morning she leaves the house without
A list, because it was in her head, just as
She went swimming in the Baleares, without
A suit. He had been envious of her, naked
In the Mediterranean, as we all wish to be,
As in a bath, she bathed as he read to her—
Renard the Fox, or something similar.

She wasn't listening it seemed to him,
She was watching little surges of past jet past
Like bats flushed from a cave.
In fact she was remembering seeing
Not a martyr's feet, but
A hair from the beard of the Prophet,
In the Topkapi, years ago, thinking
Just about anything
Looks good under glass.

At Port Royal

Should the heel of a shoe cry out
When separated from the body?
Dancing, you must think
Where to put your feet.
Too much and too little wine
(Maybe palm wine) says
Even the Grand Turk can find
The answer in a certain Italian book.

Girdle, beard, burnt hair.
Prophets think in figures,
Sins of taking things literally
When the two of everything are invisible.
Signs and effects, combinations of miracles,
They cross their arms and watch
Young ciphers learn to shimmy,
Never hear King Alpha's song.

Without such a counterweight—
Double laws, double figures, double captivity.
Imagine a body of thinking members,
How they would pray to be kept on.
Sometimes too near or faraway-eyed,
We come close to it—Casuistry. Perpetuity.
Novelty. One opinion against another.
Mangrove, et cetera.

If anyone said . . .
The illuminations did us harm.
I attacked you on behalf of others.
At Port Royal we maintain five propositions,
Six fathers, and six orients at the beginning of six ages—
That all the alms-boxes of Saint-Merry can be opened.
That an arm is as good as a foot or six-gun.
This is how Diana can be used.

In the day (that thou eatest thereof),
In a treatise on the vacuum,
The same river flowing over there
Is *numerically identical* to the same
River flowing in China. River of Babylon.
Escobar, master of conjugal acts, prove night is noon.
By their fruit, feigned peace remove.
So you are in this civil war.

At Port Royal II

Hide in the throng
To mask and disguise nature.
This shocking youth—
Paisley boy. Rude boy. Soldier boy.
Custom is nature? Excuse me, please.
Soon they will all go to Herod.
He will say you cannot
Get there from here.

Little Desdemona,
She gazes you red.
To a man,
Ratchet in pocket,
She says no no no.
Then, curvy as the tree
Outside her window,
She says yes yes yes.

Snare and gin and stumbling stone—
Only in Pharaoh and his Pharisees
Do such extremes touch and join.
Unbeliefs mate at the hip.
In times of unrule, no miracles.
Reason on its side is wicked.
We all travel across the water,
At night, go to dance.

Fish Factory in Astrakhan

Hooray, the idealistic charmer,
Viktor, has finally committed suicide!
Trapped inside a mustard
Plaster all these past four years,
Gone to seed in the eyes of God,
We patiently trace the parallel rise
And fall
Of the bosom
Of Our Lady.
Of Fatima,
Nothing is heard.
Sounds of monochromatic abandon
Prefigure the bodice, the figure skates,
Ice horizon, blatant disregard,
Then poverty.
O how we had to knuckle down,
And then some!

Five scenes later, our spindly iconoclast,
No longer a chrysalis in damask,
Breathes life into the forgotten schema:

Poor innocent seamstress becomes
Monster of depravity, archangel, mistress,
Slip-of-the-tongue doldrum ingenue
Her Calvalry
Here resurrected, FIN.

Last Vertigos

Hugo van der Goes and the Galapagos
What are you doing on Earth
And where are you going?
Though the guests are still arriving
The party is not over
It soon will be in the mind
A mental picture
To be replayed
In the last cinema where one can smoke
Certain fading embers
Exchange favors in the dark
Recalling how they once ignited
Why was no verdict reached
By yonder far bridge
Where dies were cast and suns set
So many ice floes ago
In an extinct foundry
Almost too good for Vulcan?
Go-Go Nesbitt was there
Her surrealist wonder-boy boyfriend
Emerging from three halcyon weeks
Behind drawn shades
There is no fog. This is fall, 1960
His favorite time of year. He wrote
An ode to it, many pages
An autumn almanac we now
Live inside, other side of the tracks
A little goes a long way
In folios dedicated to the vernacular

Footnotes. Someone is coming
Parallel lives and uses of Rome
Voices from the antiphone overleaf
Cicero as a boy reading a verso
Recto, treachery in the letter S
Eclogues and natural histories
In pagan Antiquity
Effort is ever more crucial

The Seventeen Points

Move and remove the darkened light
Reach for a manmade point in space
Ink in the tabula rasa
The point of departure you return to
Point of translucent crisis
Point of ellipsis, point of lacuna
Turning point, end point
Point of patina, your point exactly
Point on the map where highways end
Aka Point Fear, Point Blank
"Little Five Points"

Them Blue Lakes

Don't sweat it.
We are trapped in the same June,
Between dais and floor.
Hands of fate are rarely slight,
And if an imbroglio is a confused heap,
We are nothing more
Than beautiful stereo ripples
Whose colors give themselves away,
Imploring certain envoys
To finish their search and come home.
Here it is never winter.
Sounds amplify simply
In faraway alpine reservoirs.
Thaw comes before the deluge,
Not after, never after, the snowdrift.
A palm, waves, a caesura, many caesuras.
The object is the hardest part, lost as
Soon as others finally arrive and find
A point zero or a locus solus.
This is all we came here for.
The secret is kept up in the ozone.
Somewhere near the Hesperides
Or the Southern Cross,
Someone laughs heartily as his or her breath
Looses its way through the jetstream,
Learning and unlearning this semi-divine
Process of miscellany and diaspora
By which we seldom now daydream to conjure home.

On this nether shore
We call the ocean "Pacific,"
The girl, "Roger."
This atoll
On which we stand
Will be named later.

Something Celadon

If we trade in this *grisaille* world, can we get something celadon, or perhaps in the mint green of China? If our horse finishes first, we may choose the early Kodacolor™ of weekends and childhood vacations, in which the marlin over the bar is as three-dimensional as the Creature of the Black Lagoon, which was hardly black but emerald and full of lilypads since it was really only a rich man's idea of an Orinico, enshrined in a Southern Californian arboretum open daily.

On a backlot, Orpheus wanders through in search of the next Rob Roy in a sort of technicolor half-life flirting safely with the demimonde. This was not the kind of space we had in mind, but it will have to do. Years go by as we wear the shoes that fit, not because turnabout is fair play and the tune is "Red River Valley," nor because we dine nightly at the Peace Hotel, but simply because the motor is running and well oiled.

Stone-Deaf, Albert Leaves the Concertina

All things being equal in this reservoir
Stone-deaf Albert left the concertina
With a wave vanishing into the arcane
He embraced the hoi-polloi with relish
Watching them, too, embrace him back, for no reason
Simply because it was a rainy summer
Everyone was happy only at night
When the light at the end of the proverb
Was a house afire
And imperial garb bore
No resemblance to the throne
Sparks of revolution kindled in the garderobe
Altering the popular mood and irrigating it
Soon stylish coups became common among the populus
Incubi and succubi turned politicos
And rain washed the empty street

Fly-by shootings were everyday affairs
Especially near the rotunda
From which Albert left each dawn
June saw many fall victim needlessly
Headlines of the dailies read
MAYOR THANKS FLAK JACKET
SOONER OR LATER
ALBERT WILL PAY FOR EVIL WAYS

Sooner than later, pay he did
In the swill of the motorcade
A dozen parties formed
In the small capital of our vast archipelago

The garderobe became a thermidor
Of seething towards the poor figure
Who embraced his assassins
Knowing his time had come
The pimpled archduke, something of a cliché,
Leapt aboard the running boards
Of the Hispano-Suiza and drew his Browning
And with one shot to the head
The great man was gone

In the dénouement, as if on cue
We moved forward in the century
Beginning to read again
Inventing new forms of opera
As well as radio plays. Some summer nights
Those of us now older recalled the great man
Always dressed immaculately
Slightly jaded, something of a ham, but
A man of state nonetheless, of many liaisons

Weekend

Hell-bent for damaged goods are you mistah
Equating the lake with the surrounding bricolage
Be still while you kindly taste the scarab
Devoting fame and fortune to the caryatid
Ornery so ornery are those who idle in this portico
Madam has seen better days than phlegmatic Belgium
Echoing the succor of the tasteless anodyne
Riding the listless phalanx of warm fur (myrrh)
O wily one who topples the domino
Send notice of all future matinées

Wing

for Simon Kilmurry

Among cool recesses of tombs,
Scale models of funeral barges,
Ebony birds and mummified dogs,
A wall of tiny, broken frescos
Depicting cows in high relief,
A recumbent calf, legs in low relief,
A bull followed by a man,
Men walking left, three animals walking right,
A bearded Nubian with rope, men roping cattle,
Men with baboons, three men carrying animals,
Nubians hunting in the desert below,
Hunting with dogs, trapping birds,
Women walking left and right, women
Kneeling, with pink skin,
Crocodiles in the reeds,
Slaves cutting hops, scythes
Bent to the sun, graining
With the eye of Horus, watching
Representations of Mekutra and wife make
Offerings—figs, ducks, cucumbers, a wig,
Necklaces, unguents, a kilt, a foot—
Henenu holds the beer jar to his lips, his sons
To the right, knaves in jars, go to besiege a fortress,
Men climb scaffolding, the festival of Mia,
Porter and archer slaughter bulls,
Bows on stands as in the tomb of Neferu,
An official, the goddess Nekhet,

Symbol of Abydos and janus-type cows,
Acacia tree with vessels below it,
On the cornice above, related to the Osiris cult,
Cattle walk left with women attendants,
Carrying sunshades and menat necklaces, the queen
Faces them, her name written nearby,
Looking on while three
Priests recite spells,
Three men in kilts carrying birds
March silently forward
Through a false door with blue frame,
A false door with yellow frame,
A false door with red frame,
As the Festival escapes
Through alcoves, mezzanines, and porticos,
Sculpture galleries and rooms of armor,
Through teahouses of Old Japan,
Across Attic capitals and vases,
Kilted men watch Nebuchadnezzar eating grass
Like oxen, Magi bear birds by the Eastern Star,
Tempt Saint Anthony in the desert,
The Lion of Nemea, Job on his dunghill,
The Masters of Osservanza and the Griggs Crucifixion,
Kachina dolls and wood totems from Malindi,
All to become bearded warriors
Rushing to battle in Assyrian chariots with
Oriflammes of dreams foretold by angels,
Flagellations, annunciations, and ascensions,
Racing headlong through French woods, hounds baying,
Centurions offering birds to peasants sleeping

In the fields at noon, through the afternoon,
The lily-white model gazes hand under chin
Toward the slope of Mont Sainte-Victoire,
An earthenware jar shattering, browns and greens
Spilling into the valley below—
Vineyards, farmhouses, olive trees, and viaducts—
Over the tops of trees and the horizon line,
From L'Estaque, clear but distant,
As far as the eye can see she sees

Kilted men, some carrying birds

Keep Gieseking

for Charles North

Please write if you saw the laundromat explode
For as *The Marble Faun* wanders aimlessly through the
      firmament
So too do martens in the field sweep knowingly through
      the grass
The small town barker leads the band through town
All hear the sonic boom at night
Winters never tell where they dine
All hands on deck are put to sea
Urination is the next best thing to being there, for dogs
How could you possibly rent *Crossing Delancey*?
Be careful with that bassinet, Yvonne
To change the course of history from the piano
You must keep Gieseking from the clarinet

Scene of an Ancient Ambush

Just as cedars are known to kill snakes with their odors
Silvester not only welcomed him to his house
But introduced him to the as of yet
A green so green it is blue and yellow and seldom seen
Rendered sightless he saddled the horse and rode it
    fearlessly to the mountain
He took the mountain by storm and brought it back to a
    woman on the verge of conversion
She did not want the gift of constancy he offered her
    and so chastened he gave it instead to a wolf
Who was chased by a crow who drove him into the sea
    with the beating of its wings
Whence the poor man's corpse sank to the bottom and
    was devoured by marine monsters
Who heard a great voice and began to regret their
    actions as only do those who inhabit evil
As the sum of the divining rod curls and dims the tiny
    fires so they asked you before they departed
To the far shore, this purgatory, which is but a temporal
    resting place, a fragment of a broken vessel
In the arms of time the worms and wounds inflicted
    upon him diminished mightily, his spirit was great,
    he slept the sleep of the just
As an eloquent breath blew airlessly past the counselling
    tongue past the long channels of the rivers
Shapely as noiseless planks all concurred with the august
    reasoning from up high
While forty steps from the pit, a wagon was brought
    round for each family, each an octave

Of devoted vermillion palm cypress cedar olive a flock
    slumbering happily knowing it is safe from wolves
She was on her way back from the camels when a girl came to
    tempt her lest she not prefer to retire to a solitary life
There are but three movements of the body and two are silent
The third is the hand peeling the apple
Driven from place of shame to place of shame on a kind of sled
After his sleep, he awoke his mind full of the second principle
A great and ancient anger rose within him, a wild vigor which
    steeled and girded him
To defend the vineyard and not yield the basilica
Or the level bridge. He drove many foes into the river, raining
Blows upon them as an arrow dipped in poison
Pierced his cheek he fell and was gathered up by the enemy
Neither converted by admonitions nor frightened by marvels
He was whipped and beaten, mangled until his bones showed
Through the torn flesh. So black was his humiliation that he
Disappeared into it, and so expiring, was rescued by it
His restive soul borne on the air to the interior
The only remnant a distant wailing
Left there to prefigure the legend

Pictures of Llewellyn

I. History

The birth of Llewellyn. Llewellyn's distant past. Llewellyn from its humblest beginnings. Llewellyn under the aboriginals. Llewellyn in the time of the native coastal tribes. Llewellyn: a natural harbor. Captain Cook and the first settlers. Llewellyn and its early penal colonies. The spread of smallpox and venereal disease in early colonial Llewellyn. Abandon hope: the leper colony at Sanssouci. O cursed town: a study of early Llewellyn. Llewellyn's mythical Roman past. Llewellyn's witchhunters. Llewellyn's Huguenots. Llewellyn reborn. Llewellyn and the rise of the whaling trade. Trade winds bless Llewellyn. Llewellyn, my Llewellyn: a history in verse. The golden age of Llewellyn. Llewellyn in the machine age. Llewellyn and the age of empire. Llewellyn in the wars of independence. Llewellyn: a new Manchester? Llewellyn and the arts & crafts movement. Llewellyn and the gothic revival. Llewellyn and the Universal Exposition of 1901. Patterns of Chinese and Indian immigration in pre-war Llewellyn. Boys to men: the Llewellyn fusiliers in the Great War. Bohemian Llewellyn: origins and landmarks. Llewellyn, the fauves in. Literary Llewellyn. Joyce's Dublin and Macduff's Llewellyn. Llewellyn in the Great Depression. Llewellyn before the shark nets. Llewellyn and the gymnosophist movement. Llewellyn and the tourist boom of the south coast. Sansouci Island: leper colony to nudist colony to worldclass resort. Rags to riches: Llewellyn's Cinderella story. Llewellyn: all things to all people. Llewellyn: an essay in antiphon. Llewellyn, hooliganism in latter-day. Llewellyn: what went wrong?

Secret Life

No need to hurry the unhurried
They know where they live
And are happy to reside there
Secure in the knowledge
That the goal of life is to cultivate
Chacun pour soi and sui generis

As the outsider you must not disturb
The delicate balance that they are
Untrammelled in each his and her
Own dialect, and microclimate

They say that
In some provincial towns
Like Nevers
On summer days, at noon
It is pitch black, and nothing moves
This is enough to produce a silent scream
To make one want to leave
And never look back

Knowing that all roads lead to the capital
We depart to join the life-force of the nation

Folly Chronicle

It is positively chic to live in a folly
Which is why many style victims live in one

One hundred meters above farmland
Between New Forest and the Solent
There is much to see and do in and around
Flights of steps given free rein
To come to an abrupt halt
What a vista
Pier where the ferry docks
Yours is a small face
Lonely as a pool
Indeterminate as the light swell
North of the river
Sufficiently incomplete
This enclosure of sorts
With underground chambers
In partial if not total collapse
Has all the comforts of home
Plus satellite TV and mini-bar
A private garage just for you
With castellated gateway

But does this make it a folly?

Consider Exhibit A: blustery days
Of sun and rain that melt away
Notoriously fond of a pint
An outstanding maze
This man

An impossiblity of failure
Something serene crystalline
Hidden in the grass
Cargo for the iron fish
And the grotto inside
Creation of the shell artist
Shy of external show
The possibilities are threefold
Big fish, small ponds, storms and teacups
Motorway restaurant with an aeroplane in it
Collosal summerhouses that serve as reference points
Even in Leicestershire, least promising
Folly county in Britain, outlying
Garden buildings can surprise and delight
If in themselves rather undistinguished
Sporadic attacks of vandalism
Deserve mention, as does
A hearty Welsh breakfast, and the famous gazebo
Whose horse-shaped weather vane was stolen
A relative point of departure, ten kinetic effects
See them soon before the other half goes

The Folly of Love

Here I grow in a straight line
Down by the riverbank
Where in the present
Past and future merge
This pole is not a zone
Full of narrow shade
So cool so calm so bright
So pagan youth so naturally her
Temporally and spatially lost from view
Bent ear and eye that humble vale
Whose lower slope, an orchard
Some troop of words segues through
Crazy flames sprung thought lives among
The distant manchild stumbles upon
With neither sign nor government

War in a Mousetrap (Prequel)

If a blue boat is the vehicle of fools
And yellow signifies enmity, who wouldn't
Hoist the green sail of whole cloth painted twice
Whose face is not at all Italian
Divide the spheres and fortunes of the haves
And the have-nots into farflung landlocked navies
Contrapuntal if deaf to the layered rapports
Of the plastic arts? A certain flamboyant element of
High serious melancholy becoming and unbecoming
   the context
So totally lacking in evolution and variation
It did not fail to incite the crowd's derision
And so, and so until with the quick strokes of lambs' bleats
The escarpment was mounted and diverted anew
Between the white foliate earth and the mountain
Product of the less than desirable abject quintessence of
   celestial azure hue cast away
The orb starts to turn and in its revolutions begins to see
Itself an obelisk standing lonely on an embankment
While streams and brooks cross and tether themselves
   together as rivers
In new knots breaking open seams in the rock
Four myriad jeremiads soldier forth across the
   metaphysical plain
One you too once knew some time ago now
And in one Glasse must be done all thys thyng
Lyke to an Egge in shape, and closyd well

Le retour de l'homme celadon

Who serves
Green tints in wicker cups
To the many guests in white
In this long prenuptial dream
Summer thunderstorms fill the room
Whose tablecloths are the color
In which conversation floats

As Told To

This passing reference to
The sound of a car passing in the night
Sheds light on the more obvious
Angles of the possible movements of
The immense and deadly
Shadow organization
Whose formidable criminal genius
And panther-like stealth
Is now at your fingertips.

It is time to jettison the excess baggage
And open the floodlights,
Illuminating all those squatters living in the ellipses,
Not to mention the watersheds.

Yes, it is all out in the open now.
So it was you, my friend, who reduced
My soliloquies to babble
(Something akin to a brown sauce or *sauce espagnole*),
Consigning me to oblivion.
Let me let you in on a secret—
I have always wanted to be consigned to oblivion.
It is my expression of our great cultural death wish,
And, contrary to popular belief,
Oblivion is not an island whose chief port is Encomia
(Or formerly, in Roman times, Encomium),
It is a place where one can do and say as one pleases,
Where one can "move freely"
And sometimes put on airs,
Just sit around and digress all day,

Taking the scenic route,
Stand on ceremony or step down from it
Into the realm of plain talk,
Every once in a while, when needed,
Casually interjecting phrases
Like *torpid obloquy* and *pellucid freshet*.
Here you can use the royal We with impunity
And sometimes be a real ass,
Speak parenthetically yet in the moment,
Say the highly-charged stuff only
Actors get to say, like
"We know where you live,"
"Play it as it lays," and
"Steady as she goes."
(That mysterious she,
She always was a cipher.
She had to be seen to be believed,
Stealing your money, heart, lines, and thunder,
Then disappearing into summer,
Each time like the last time,
Or the first time,
It's hard to remember now.)

Bivouac

A steady rain
Defines a marked space
Like clockwork
The old world
The seventh skein
And curved time
Is its own element
An inverted mountainside
Referenced on the map
With an angled nod
Barely perceptible
To the viewer
In whose language
Of brick and vapor
Phrases suddenly turn
In on themselves
Down country lanes
In other parts of the world
Where the dream of the map
Charts the long rain and the mountain
The spot where the suitor was transfixed
And let go in the next unfolding
Too can be seen
Groups of small details
Evolving into motifs of face value
Progressively refined
In the broad lines
Of the mature style
For the sake of argument
Whose hidden motives

Are so purely and utterly
Erotic, as is the whole
Of the scenario
Illuminated in the distance
In the last of the war canoes
Accord is reached, in effect
If memory serves
Before rain stops play
At least in impression
A measure of variation
Left to drift awhile
Always well to the right
Of the vortex
An area of low pressure
Dangerous valence
Where parallels are recognizable
Easily compared
To the round head
And her bell-like shape
Which is everywhere
And the analogous trees
Who in their magic qualities are
Coevals to the universal
Poised to move beyond
Taking star turns in mid-flight
This victory of the double subject
Fleeting at best, is
Midwife to certain shapes
And forms who must return
By the onset to offset
The middle passage, by definition

A tenuous equilibrium
One redolent of deception
Whose only vital function is
Momentary, to shadow and mirror
The central paradox
Once part of the solution
Such unfamiliar ground held
Clues to the delicate balance
The guise of foreignness
So the maxim goes
Largely unembellished
If somewhat apocryphal
In its bare facts, a profile
In retrospect, the prospect
Of a lake, suggested outlines
Of the female figure, at least
The technical part of it
In any case, by all accounts
An ingenious use of *trompe l'œil*
With few regrets, the boat embarks
A serene and final detachment
To burden the stillness of the air
In circumscribed orbits
Along vanishing borders
To the previous forest

Back on Our Heads

In the moment
That those pointed firs
Which comprise the deep
And wild fir forest
Bend into view
Inclining with a nod
Quaver and shiver
To remind you
        you must always
Sleep with the greenfinches
When basking with Dryads
Or wandering the constellations
Of dark marshes where chance
Is shown the door
        you once knew
How to enhance the unwithering palm
Then prune it of all faults
To write *scarlet* for *candida*
And ink the ladder for
Pallid cadillacs of empty fire

Sketches from *A Brief History of the Low Countries*

Before the Middle Ages
The delta of the great rivers
Was not subsumed by name
For the Low Countries
The fragmentation was very great

I. *Sluys*

The former port, how does it feel,
Now that it is an empty market town,
Five miles inland? Is it angry,
Or wistful, the way that Antwerp was
When Amsterdam forced her
To close her quays along the Scheldt,
Knowing her golden age was up?
Speaking of the Scheldt and silt,
Perhaps we should ask poor Sluys,
Where English raiders sacked
The French Armada centuries ago.
She might ask her sister towns,
For instance, Aigues-Mortes,
Where Louis departed for the Holy Land,
Or Miletus and Priene, formerly
Facing each other across a sizeable bay,
Now farmland, courtesy the River Meander.

II. *Uitlander*

These thoughts are far
From the mind
Of the delivery man
Whistling a Boney M song
As he drives his milk van
Across the polder.
This man cannot dream in Spanish,
But has he been to Paris, Milan, or Genoa?
Does he have a nephew in the other Batavia,
Halfway around the globe?
At the very least, is he
Handy on a ship?
Of sturdy stock he is, and
Dutch, he must be, for the Dutch
Have always known their way around
On and beside the water.

III. *Inlander*

The relation between the embroidered drape,
Stubbornly revealing scenes from the hunt,
And the map of the canalled city,
Surrounded by merchants' homes,
Is the same as between
The parquet floor and
Raftered ceiling.
The girl holds a sackbut
In one hand, a book in the other
Her eyes are closed, her hair sprouting

Forest floors of the New World, she seems
Ready to exit into white, behind the drape.
The portraitist, however, is just starting out.
His feet are splayed,
A crossroads, the easel, a taut bow
Aimed at the canalled city, a web of cross-hairs
Warmly but dimly remembered
In myopic detail. She smiles,
Head faltering as a cornucopia.
Contrapuntal to the modest chandelier,
An oversized mask lies dead on the table,
Emulating a pheasant. Shadows hide
Shiny rivets. Even so, the mood is serene.
It is winter, early afternoon.

IV. *St. Odulphuskerk*

In the old as in the new
A pastel silence is dissolving
Into the white
Even shadows
Finding home
Dog beside him
A townsman
Pipe in mouth
Gossips with two women
Nodding as far off
Like birds
Tiny black heads rise
Above the pews
Floating upward

Past the cables
Arcs and buttresses
Toward the sunlit vaults

V. *In Delft*

We know the figures on the riverbank.
They are from the so-called Papenhoek,
Or Papists' Corner. (And you wondered why
The girls all look like nuns!) Somber
As the dead water, William
The Silent, Prince of Orange,
The cloud in the foreground,
Is set to rain on our heads,
The one beyond is cirrus
And full of sun. Counterfeit, we
Inherit the inn, and must convert.
The lower steeples are in shadow.
Ocher stone in early debt
Protects the market square, sufficiently
Prosperous, a town lovingly hated
As a distant relative, expires
By the river, red roofs at left, a map
Already outdated at the time of this work—
Seventeen not seven provinces—
There is nothing left this town.

VI. *The Master of the Rocky Landscape*

October and its rock outcroppings
Are subtly alluded to somewhere
Near the Meuse en route to the journey
Across the Alps to Italy the blind man
And his guide are tiny figures just this side
Of the sloping wood beyond which a lion
Is charging the returning herd in a patch
Of sun a different lion than the one
At the feet of the barefoot Jerome
Inside his shady hideaway a cave
Inside a rocky outcrop atop which rests
A scale model of some cathedral
Not of Dinant home of the artist
But perhaps of Brussels or Antwerp in the far
A large inlet is an arm of the sea
Flecked with sea traffic a storm is approaching
From the west beyond giant rock outcroppings
Like mountains of the moon the Alps the Sinai
Patinate vestiges of the artist's childhood
In Dinant by the river Meuse

VII. *J.H.*

Inside he looks outside
The even landscape is green
And wet and unchanged
He stays inside
Under house arrest, and ill
Stomach empty, body failing
Mind still full of many things
Time for one last book
Many possible topics
A history of potlatch
Etymologies of Sanskrit
The years in Leiden
On being Freisian
Claus Sluiter
More on the adoration
Of detail
Or the violent tenor of life?
No, no, no, and no
Instead he writes
A book about America,
Wall Street and
Hollywood mostly,
As outside
Some shells
Begin falling

Orange Tangent

Pattern baldness in the landed gentry
Once removed is twice removed
Until at a certain remove it becomes remote
A place of comfort only to scorpions
Desert hermits, and the odd rabbit or deer
Crouching in the stony wind tunnel
Hic sunt leones
Like the stylite whose mind soon went
They are mere hiccups, wow and flutter
Amidst the empty shale, though even there
The rich patterns that life throws up
Every so often are delirious and beautiful
Ready to run off with some cute stranger
At the drop of a hat, like a faucet left on
A vast similitude interlocks all,
And after many years of intervals
Suddenly there is duration. Multitudes
Crowd into the emptiness, the prima materia
Once so obdurate, receives all
In the folds of a mercurial sea
The marinated king nearly drowns
Yet is saved, renewed, and united
With his better half, in a chemical wedding
And the hunt for the green lion is on

His Kind of Woman

Too much laughter in the dark
Can drive a man insane
Convince him to take a walk
In the park or just go
Out for a pack of cigarettes
Good trouble is hard to find
This could be the reason
We still stick together
After all these dog years
We stopped asking each
Other questions long ago
Certain things make no sense
While other things are still burning
Like a string of nights in Mexico
You must remember those
Or maybe not
Was it something I said
Or something in the water
Or the air, it was always the air
A certain color you could never
Put your finger on
However much you tried

Cheap Day Return

Underlying your feet

The floor appears to extend under our own feet

Gently undulating patches

Show us St. Jerome in a real "cabinet"

Of cloud, blue, and field

We ourselves have been admitted into it

Brown and green, telephone lines

Like nearly all Italian interiors

Blur, fold in two whites

Put this ambivalent method to use

Slow curve of earth

The 90° rotation of the whole world

Train of birds

Not the space as such

Steeple or two, behind a copse

A turning movement

Bare trees, football pitch

A round dance

Drenched with rain, hay bales

Entirely different from the North

Several tractors, sheep, cows

The claim of the object

Abandoned hanger, olive drab

Encounters

Power station, drainage canal

The ambition of the subject

Sudden downpour (flooding was predicted)

Like free will

Cemetery, silos, clearing

The central vanishing point

The distance some miles away

The traditional gold ground

A motorway, moving faster

Best placed, in real dimensions

Cut timber, hedgerows, fields

Still common in the Trecento

Newly tilled, pasture, swans

Altdorfer used just such a view

Gulls, old woman in large field

To dissolve the bodies

Hillside, in and out, wisps of smoke

Introducing an accidental

Slide, council houses

Factor to limit

Teeter-totter, burning refuse

The limiting

Farmer, reservoir, cathedral

Shed all vestiges of

Spire, beehives, a grove

An antique continuum

Clearing, chopped down trees

Overtly completing the break

Headland, water tower, rainstorm

Systems of lax fixity

Greenhouse, geese, bending as decoys

The elevation of the pyramid

Industrial park, rail sheds, dog legs

Left of the dilettante Alberti

Caravan homes, poultry shack

Each strip of floor

Scrub oak, windsock, safety orange

Diminishes

Horse, watchman's hut, fen

By one third

Crow, rain, window

Two generations later

Mud, land rover, propane tank

The desired depth intervals

Steel mill, cooling towers, combine

Fold back

Gravel pit, headlight, postal van

To plasticity

Milkman, watchcap, tennis court

A checkerboard pattern

Airstrip, glider, tour bus

Of so-called transversals

Estuary, furlough, clothesline

Rein and rudder

Multiglass, potting shed, brickyard

Certain orthogonals

Gasworks, windmill, footpath

Converging amidst them

Protractor, transit, scaffolding

Tools for the planar section

Saw mill, loading dock

In which they both rest

Junction, generator, to let

Rest in the same way

Hazard light, man at work

Unambiguous and consistent

Golf course, donkey, cowpen

Create a fishbone effect

Flood waters, scarecrow, delivery van

Of light and dark

Blue sky, scudding clouds

Embrace and dissolve

Flyover, grange, labrador

Reversals of bodies

Barn, rain, sun

And nonbodies

Text set in Perpetua. Titles are in Monotype Abadi.
The front cover design features a curve discovered
by René de Sluze, given the name "Pearls of Sluze"
by Blaise Pascal.